D1301867

Heroes for Young Readers

Written by Renee Taft Meloche
Illustrated by Bryan Pollard

Adoniram Judson	Gladys Aylward
Amy Carmichael	Hudson Taylor
Betty Greene	Jim Elliot
Cameron Townsend	Jonathan Goforth
Corrie ten Boom	Lottie Moon
David Livingstone	Mary Slessor
Eric Liddell	Nate Saint
George Müller	William Carey

Heroes of History for Young Readers

Written by Renee Taft Meloche
Illustrated by Bryan Pollard

Clara Barton
George Washington
George Washington Carver
Meriwether Lewis

…and more coming soon

*Heroes for Young Readers Activity Guides and audio CDs
are now available! See the back of this book for more information.*

For a free catalog of books and materials contact
YWAM Publishing, P.O. Box 55787, Seattle, WA 98155
1-800-922-2143, www.ywampublishing.com

HEROES OF HISTORY FOR YOUNG READERS

GEORGE WASHINGTON

America's Patriot

Written by Renee Taft Meloche
Illustrated by Bryan Pollard

Emerald Books
P.O. BOX 635
LYNNWOOD, WA 98046

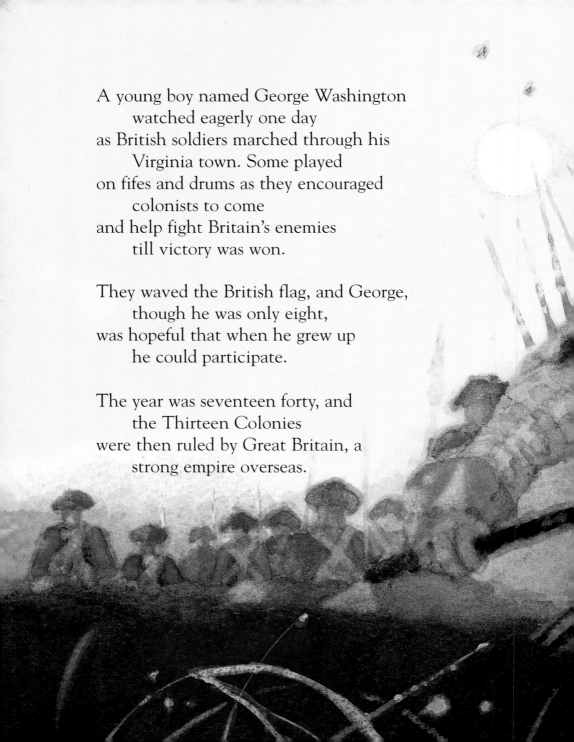

A young boy named George Washington
    watched eagerly one day
as British soldiers marched through his
    Virginia town. Some played
on fifes and drums as they encouraged
    colonists to come
and help fight Britain's enemies
    till victory was won.

They waved the British flag, and George,
    though he was only eight,
was hopeful that when he grew up
    he could participate.

The year was seventeen forty, and
    the Thirteen Colonies
were then ruled by Great Britain, a
    strong empire overseas.

George loved to ride on horseback;
    he galloped very fast.
He read a lot and liked to hunt
    and went to fencing class.

He grew into a sturdy man,
    tall and athletic too.
And soon his childhood dream to fight
    with British troops came true.

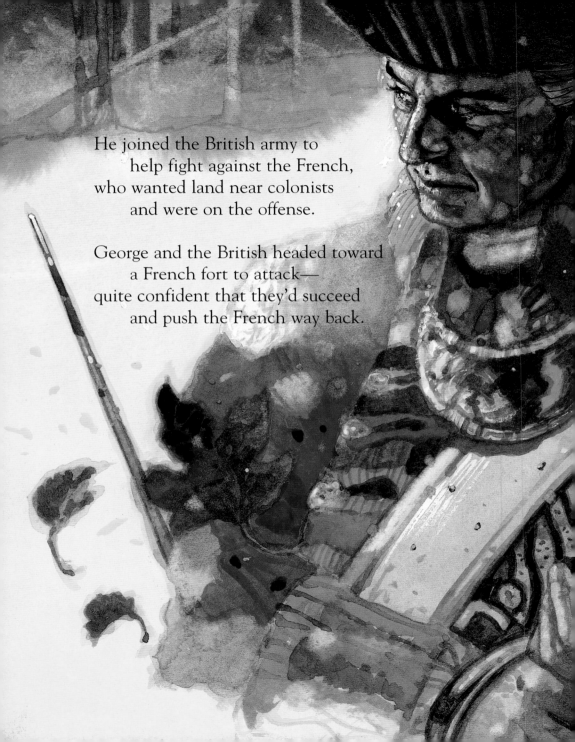

He joined the British army to
    help fight against the French,
who wanted land near colonists
    and were on the offense.

George and the British headed toward
    a French fort to attack—
quite confident that they'd succeed
    and push the French way back.

Because George was the general's aide,
    he rode his horse behind
the British soldiers, who were marching
    neatly in straight lines.

These British "redcoats" all held muskets
    gleaming in the light,
and all were unaware an ambush
    was just out of sight.

Some Indians, helped by the French,
    were hiding with their guns
and suddenly began to shoot
    the soldiers one by one.

The redcoats—easy targets—made
    George beg the general, "Please!
Allow the men to scatter, sir,
    behind the rocks and trees."

"That's not the British way," he said,
    and soon they were defeated.
Two horses that George rode were killed
    before they all retreated.

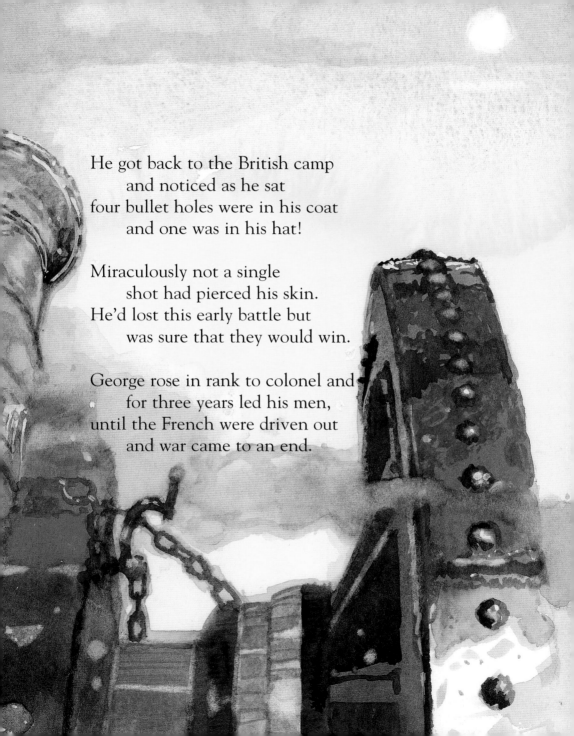

He got back to the British camp
    and noticed as he sat
four bullet holes were in his coat
    and one was in his hat!

Miraculously not a single
    shot had pierced his skin.
He'd lost this early battle but
    was sure that they would win.

George rose in rank to colonel and
    for three years led his men,
until the French were driven out
    and war came to an end.

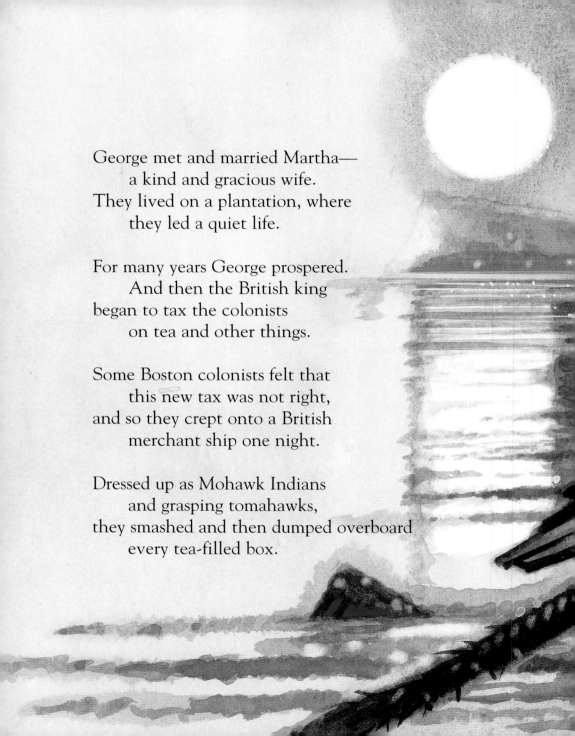

George met and married Martha—
    a kind and gracious wife.
They lived on a plantation, where
    they led a quiet life.

For many years George prospered.
    And then the British king
began to tax the colonists
    on tea and other things.

Some Boston colonists felt that
    this new tax was not right,
and so they crept onto a British
    merchant ship one night.

Dressed up as Mohawk Indians
    and grasping tomahawks,
they smashed and then dumped overboard
    every tea-filled box.

It was not long before George heard
     a very bad report:
the British king—now furious—
     had closed the Boston port.

This stopped all work on ships, which meant
     that many lost their jobs.
The colonists were really mad—
     they felt like they'd been robbed.

Soon Pennsylvanians, Georgians, and
     Virginians—others, too—
joined hands as one: *Americans.*
     This common name was new.

The Thirteen Colonies elected
        men they thought were bright
to talk about these unjust acts
        and whether they should fight.

When George was chosen, he and Martha
        spent the day in prayer.
They asked God for His wisdom and
        to help them to prepare.

Before too long the leaders saw
        that they must go to war
against the very nation they
        were members of before.

Promoted now to general, George
led sixteen thousand men
from thirteen different colonies
who now had to defend
themselves against the British—more
equipped and better trained.
And if George failed, his men would be
called traitors and be hanged.

Because his men were untrained and
their weapons were too few,
George worked to get them disciplined
before the year was through.

They drove the British out of Boston
so effectively
the British hired Hessian soldiers—
feared from Germany!

Meanwhile, a document was signed
    that claimed equality
and freedom for Americans
    to live in liberty.

This Independence Declaration
    signed on July fourth
in seventeen hundred seventy-six
    is why they went to war.

In New York harbor British warships
    landed troops on shore.
The men George led, called "patriots,"
    were pushed back more and more.

The Hessians, who had joined the British,
    were a fearsome threat.
The patriots fought bravely with
    their guns and bayonets.

However, they were still outmatched,
    so on a foggy night
George knew he had to move his soldiers
    farther out of sight.

It was Manhattan Island where
    George and his men now stayed.
He readied them again for battle
    in the coming days.

Weeks later, when they were attacked,
    things did not go as planned.
This time the patriots got scared
    and would not fight—they ran!

Though disappointed in his men,
    George rallied them again.
As summer turned to fall, though, things
    looked hopeless, bleak, and grim.

The redcoats chased the troops like foxes
    through small towns and woods.
George and his men escaped each time:
    they fought the best they could.

The patriots pushed on across
        the river Delaware
and into Pennsylvania, feeling
        hunger, cold, despair.

Since it was wintertime, the British
        thought it would be best
to finish fighting in the spring.
        Until then they would rest.

As Christmas neared, the patriots
        all wanted to go home.
Their shoes were worn; they had no capes;
        they shivered to the bone.

The soldiers had signed up till year's
        end—only days away.
A victory was needed to
        convince enough to stay.

Around the campsite George decided
        his men should surprise
the Hessians camped across the river
        on the other side.

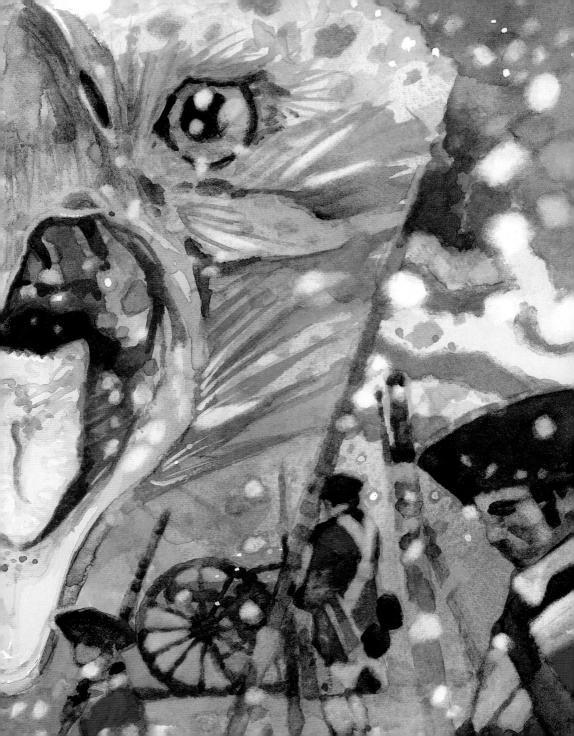

On Christmas Day he led his cold,
    exhausted, hungry men
across the icy river as
    a blizzard raged round them.

They walked for miles in the snow
    with rags wrapped on their feet.
They slipped and bled but yet pressed on,
    refusing to retreat.

Then on December twenty-sixth
    George ordered them to strike.
The Hessians scrambled from their tents,
    not ready for a fight.

They grabbed their coats and rifles, tripped
    and stumbled on the ground.
The cannons of the patriots
    cut many Hessians down.

The others soon surrendered; George
    had known what was at stake.
Yet he had risked it all to stand
    and fight for freedom's sake.

Then many soldiers reenlisted,
    though they'd planned to go,
and France now joined America
    to fight their common foe.

And after years of dreadful war,
    in seventeen eighty-one,
Great Britain then surrendered: young
    America had won!

When George retired as commander,
    some were questioning,
"Why doesn't he seize power now
    and rule as our new king?"

Wise George knew that America
    must not be ruled that way,
but rather governed by the people,
    who'd all have a say.

They'd need a government to keep
    peace at home and abroad,
to pay the nation's debts and help
    the people set up laws.

So George and others wrote a constitution
    that provided
the laws to help the people rule
    and to stay undivided.

They chose to have a president,
    a man equipped to lead.
They wanted George, and with much thought,
    he finally agreed.

He took a horse-drawn carriage to
    New York, and as he neared,
the people lined his path with petals,
    greeting him with cheers.

Their war hero was back again
    and now would lead them on;
he'd help them keep their freedom and
    help make their nation strong.

George took the oath of office, then,
    in seventeen eighty-nine:
he held the Bible, kissed it too,
    and city church bells chimed.

He stayed in office for two terms,
    and when eight years had passed,
he felt his service to his country
    was complete at last.

George Washington gave up his power
    voluntarily.
No leader in the world had ever
    done that willingly.

The world was so surprised Great Britain's
    king had this to say:
"George is the greatest character
    of this entire age."

In seventeen ninety-nine George died.
    Americans all mourned.
Because he'd led with courage, a
    great nation had been born.

He paved the way for others and
    he showed them how to lead.
This honored patriot helped found
    a land of liberty.

Christian Heroes: Then & Now

by Janet and Geoff Benge

Adoniram Judson: Bound for Burma
Amy Carmichael: Rescuer of Precious Gems
Betty Greene: Wings to Serve
Brother Andrew: God's Secret Agent
Cameron Townsend: Good News in Every Language
Clarence Jones: Mr. Radio
Corrie ten Boom: Keeper of the Angels' Den
Count Zinzendorf: Firstfruit
C.T. Studd: No Retreat
David Livingstone: Africa's Trailblazer
Eric Liddell: Something Greater Than Gold
Florence Young: Mission Accomplished
George Müller: The Guardian of Bristol's Orphans
Gladys Aylward: The Adventure of a Lifetime
Hudson Taylor: Deep in the Heart of China
Ida Scudder: Healing Bodies, Touching Hearts
Jim Elliot: One Great Purpose
John Williams: Messenger of Peace
Jonathan Goforth: An Open Door in China
Lillian Trasher: The Greatest Wonder in Egypt
Loren Cunningham: Into All the World
Lottie Moon: Giving Her All for China
Mary Slessor: Forward into Calabar
Nate Saint: On a Wing and a Prayer
Rachel Saint: A Star in the Jungle
Rowland Bingham: Into Africa's Interior
Sundar Singh: Footprints Over the Mountains
Wilfred Grenfell: Fisher of Men
William Booth: Soup, Soap, and Salvation
William Carey: Obliged to Go

Heroes for Young Readers and Heroes of History for Young Readers are based on the Christian Heroes: Then & Now and Heroes of History biographies by Janet and Geoff Benge. Don't miss out on these exciting, true adventures for ages ten and up!

Continued on the next page...

Heroes of History

by Janet and Geoff Benge

Abraham Lincoln: A New Birth of Freedom
Benjamin Franklin: Live Wire
Christopher Columbus: Across the Ocean Sea
Clara Barton: Courage under Fire
Daniel Boone: Frontiersman
Douglas MacArthur: What Greater Honor
George Washington Carver: From Slave to Scientist
George Washington: True Patriot
Harriet Tubman: Freedombound
John Adams: Independence Forever
John Smith: A Foothold in the New World
Laura Ingalls Wilder: A Storybook Life
Meriwether Lewis: Off the Edge of the Map
Orville Wright: The Flyer
Theodore Roosevelt: An American Original
William Penn: Liberty and Justice for All

...and more coming soon. Unit study curriculum guides are also available.

Heroes for Young Readers Activity Guides
Educational and Character-Building Lessons for Children
by Renee Taft Meloche

Heroes for Young Readers Activity Guide for Books 1–4
Gladys Aylward, Eric Liddell, Nate Saint, George Müller

Heroes for Young Readers Activity Guide for Books 5–8
Amy Carmichael, Corrie ten Boom, Mary Slessor, William Carey

Heroes for Young Readers Activity Guide for Books 9–12
Betty Greene, David Livingstone, Adoniram Judson, Hudson Taylor

Heroes for Young Readers Activity Guide for Books 13–16
Jim Elliot, Cameron Townsend, Jonathan Goforth, Lottie Moon

...and more coming soon.

Designed to accompany the vibrant Heroes for Young Readers books, these fun-filled activity guides lead young children through a variety of character-building and educational activities. Pick and choose from the activities or follow the included thirteen-week syllabus. An audio CD with book readings, songs, and fun activity tracks is available for each Activity Guide.

For a free catalog of books and materials contact
YWAM Publishing, P.O. Box 55787, Seattle, WA 98155
1-800-922-2143, www.ywampublishing.com